SEAMUS HEANEY

Death of a Naturalist

ff

faber and faber

LONDON · BOSTON

First published in 1966
by Faber and Faber Limited
3 Queen Square London WC1N 3AU
This paperback edition first published in 1969
Reprinted 1973, 1976, 1978, 1980, 1985,
1986, 1987, 1988 and 1989
Reset with amendments 1991

Photoset by Wilmaset, Birkenhead, Wirral
Printed in England by
Mackays of Chatham plc, Chatham, Kent

© Seamus Heaney, 1966, 1991

A CIP record for this book
is available from the British Library

ISBN 0 571 09024 9

8 10 9 7

For Marie

Contents

Acknowledgements are due to the editors of the following, in which some of these poems have appeared:

Belfast Telegraph, Dublin Magazine, Kilkenny Magazine, Interest, Irish Times, The Listener, New Statesman, Northern Review, Outposts, Poetry Ireland, Vogue; The Arts in Ulster (BBC Northern Ireland), *The Living Poet* and *The Poet's Voice* (BBC Third Programme); Universities Poetry 5, Young Commonwealth Poets '65 (Heinemann).

Digging

Between my finger and my thumb
The squat pen rests; snug as a gun.

Under my window, a clean rasping sound
When the spade sinks into gravelly ground:
My father, digging. I look down

Till his straining rump among the flowerbeds
Bends low, comes up twenty years away
Stooping in rhythm through potato drills
Where he was digging.

The coarse boot nestled on the lug, the shaft
Against the inside knee was levered firmly.
He rooted out tall tops, buried the bright edge deep
To scatter new potatoes that we picked,
Loving their cool hardness in our hands.

By God, the old man could handle a spade.
Just like his old man.

My grandfather cut more turf in a day
Than any other man on Toner's bog.
Once I carried him milk in a bottle
Corked sloppily with paper. He straightened up
To drink it, then fell to right away

Nicking and slicing neatly, heaving sods
Over his shoulder, going down and down
For the good turf. Digging.

The cold smell of potato mould, the squelch and slap
Of soggy peat, the curt cuts of an edge
Through living roots awaken in my head.
But I've no spade to follow men like them.

Between my finger and my thumb
The squat pen rests.
I'll dig with it.

Death of a Naturalist

All year the flax-dam festered in the heart
Of the townland; green and heavy headed
Flax had rotted there, weighted down by huge sods.
Daily it sweltered in the punishing sun.
Bubbles gargled delicately, bluebottles
Wove a strong gauze of sound around the smell.
There were dragon-flies, spotted butterflies,
But best of all was the warm thick slobber
Of frogspawn that grew like clotted water
In the shade of the banks. Here, every spring,
I would fill jampotfuls of the jellied
Specks to range on window-sills at home,
On shelves at school, and wait and watch until
The fattening dots burst into nimble-
Swimming tadpoles. Miss Walls would tell us how
The daddy frog was called a bullfrog,
And how he croaked, and how the mammy frog
Laid hundreds of little eggs and this was
Frogspawn. You could tell the weather by frogs too
For they were yellow in the sun and brown
In rain.

Then one hot day when fields were rank
With cowdung in the grass, the angry frogs
Invaded the flax-dam; I ducked through hedges
To a coarse croaking that I had not heard
Before. The air was thick with a bass chorus.
Right down the dam, gross-bellied frogs were cocked

On sods; their loose necks pulsed like sails. Some
    hopped:
The slap and plop were obscene threats. Some sat
Poised like mud grenades, their blunt heads farting.
I sickened, turned, and ran. The great slime kings
Were gathered there for vengeance, and I knew
That if I dipped my hand the spawn would clutch it.

The Barn

Threshed corn lay piled like grit of ivory
Or solid as cement in two-lugged sacks.
The musty dark hoarded an armoury
Of farmyard implements, harness, plough-socks.

The floor was mouse-grey, smooth, chilly concrete.
There were no windows, just two narrow shafts
Of gilded motes, crossing, from air-holes slit
High in each gable. The one door meant no draughts

All summer when the zinc burned like an oven.
A scythe's edge, a clean spade, a pitch-fork's prongs:
Slowly bright objects formed when you went in.
Then you felt cobwebs clogging up your lungs

And scuttled fast into the sunlit yard –
And into nights when bats were on the wing
Over the rafters of sleep, where bright eyes stared
From piles of grain in corners, fierce, unblinking.

The dark gulfed like a roof-space. I was chaff
To be pecked up when birds shot through the air-slits.
I lay face-down to shun the fear above.
The two-lugged sacks moved in like great blind rats.

An Advancement of Learning

I took the embankment path
(As always, deferring
The bridge). The river nosed past,
Pliable, oil-skinned, wearing

A transfer of gables and sky.
Hunched over the railing,
Well away from the road now, I
Considered the dirty-keeled swans.

Something slobbered curtly, close,
Smudging the silence: a rat
Slimed out of the water and
My throat sickened so quickly that

I turned down the path in cold sweat
But God, another was nimbling
Up the far bank, tracing its wet
Arcs on the stones. Incredibly then

I established a dreaded
Bridgehead. I turned to stare
With deliberate, thrilled care
At my hitherto snubbed rodent.

He clockworked aimlessly a while,
Stopped, back bunched and glistening,
Ears plastered down on his knobbled skull,
Insidiously listening.

The tapered tail that followed him,
The raindrop eye, the old snout:
One by one I took all in.
He trained on me. I stared him out

Forgetting how I used to panic
When his grey brothers scraped and fed
Behind the hen-coop in our yard,
On ceiling boards above my bed.

This terror, cold, wet-furred, small-clawed,
Retreated up a pipe for sewage.
I stared a minute after him.
Then I walked on and crossed the bridge.

Blackberry-Picking

For Philip Hobsbaum

Late August, given heavy rain and sun
For a full week, the blackberries would ripen.
At first, just one, a glossy purple clot
Among others, red, green, hard as a knot.
You ate that first one and its flesh was sweet
Like thickened wine: summer's blood was in it
Leaving stains upon the tongue and lust for
Picking. Then red ones inked up, and that hunger
Sent us out with milk-cans, pea-tins, jam-pots
Where briars scratched and wet grass bleached our
      boots.
Round hayfields, cornfields and potato-drills,
We trekked and picked until the cans were full,
Until the tinkling bottom had been covered
With green ones, and on top big dark blobs burned
Like a plate of eyes. Our hands were peppered
With thorn pricks, our palms sticky as Bluebeard's.

We hoarded the fresh berries in the byre.
But when the bath was filled we found a fur,
A rat-grey fungus, glutting on our cache.
The juice was stinking too. Once off the bush,
The fruit fermented, the sweet flesh would turn sour.
I always felt like crying. It wasn't fair
That all the lovely canfuls smelt of rot.
Each year I hoped they'd keep, knew they would not.

Churning Day

A thick crust, coarse-grained as limestone rough-cast,
hardened gradually on top of the four crocks
that stood, large pottery bombs, in the small pantry.
After the hot brewery of gland, cud and udder,
cool porous earthenware fermented the buttermilk
for churning day, when the hooped churn was
   scoured
with plumping kettles and the busy scrubber
echoed daintily on the seasoned wood.
It stood then, purified, on the flagged kitchen floor.

Out came the four crocks, spilled their heavy lip
of cream, their white insides, into the sterile churn.
The staff, like a great whisky muddler fashioned
in deal wood, was plunged in, the lid fitted.
My mother took first turn, set up rhythms
that slugged and thumped for hours. Arms ached.
Hands blistered. Cheeks and clothes were spattered

with flabby milk.
               Where finally gold flecks
began to dance. They poured hot water then,
sterilized a birchwood-bowl
and little corrugated butter-spades.
Their short stroke quickened, suddenly
a yellow curd was weighting the churned up white,
heavy and rich, coagulated sunlight
that they fished, dripping, in a wide tin strainer,
heaped up like gilded gravel in the bowl.

The house would stink long after churning day,
acrid as a sulphur mine. The empty crocks
were ranged along the wall again, the butter
in soft printed slabs was piled on pantry shelves.
And in the house we moved with gravid ease,
our brains turned crystals full of clean deal churns,
the plash and gurgle of the sour-breathed milk,
the pat and slap of small spades on wet lumps.

The Early Purges

I was six when I first saw kittens drown.
Dan Taggart pitched them, 'the scraggy wee shits',
Into a bucket; a frail metal sound,

Soft paws scraping like mad. But their tiny din
Was soon soused. They were slung on the snout
Of the pump and the water pumped in.

'Sure isn't it better for them now?' Dan said.
Like wet gloves they bobbed and shone till he sluiced
Them out on the dunghill, glossy and dead.

Suddenly frightened, for days I sadly hung
Round the yard, watching the three sogged remains
Turn mealy and crisp as old summer dung

Until I forgot them. But the fear came back
When Dan trapped big rats, snared rabbits, shot crows
Or, with a sickening tug, pulled old hens' necks.

Still, living displaces false sentiments
And now, when shrill pups are prodded to drown,
I just shrug, 'Bloody pups'. It makes sense:

'Prevention of cruelty' talk cuts ice in town
Where they consider death unnatural,
But on well-run farms pests have to be kept down.

Follower

My father worked with a horse-plough,
His shoulders globed like a full sail strung
Between the shafts and the furrow.
The horses strained at his clicking tongue.

An expert. He would set the wing
And fit the bright steel-pointed sock.
The sod rolled over without breaking.
At the headrig, with a single pluck

Of reins, the sweating team turned round
And back into the land. His eye
Narrowed and angled at the ground,
Mapping the furrow exactly.

I stumbled in his hob-nailed wake,
Fell sometimes on the polished sod;
Sometimes he rode me on his back,
Dipping and rising to his plod.

I wanted to grow up and plough,
To close one eye, stiffen my arm.
All I ever did was follow
In his broad shadow round the farm.

I was a nuisance, tripping, falling,
Yapping always. But today
It is my father who keeps stumbling
Behind me, and will not go away.

Ancestral Photograph

Jaws puff round and solid as a turnip,
Dead eyes are statue's and the upper lip
Bullies the heavy mouth down to a droop.
A bowler suggests the stage Irishman
Whose look has two parts scorn, two parts dead pan.
His silver watch chain girds him like a hoop.

My father's uncle, from whom he learnt the trade,
Long fixed in sepia tints, begins to fade
And must come down. Now on the bedroom wall
There is a faded patch where he has been –
As if a bandage had been ripped from skin –
Empty plaque to a house's rise and fall.

Twenty years ago I herded cattle
Into pens or held them against a wall
Until my father won at arguing
His own price on a crowd of cattlemen
Who handled rumps, groped teats, stood, paused and
     then
Bought a round of drinks to clinch the bargain.

Uncle and nephew, fifty years ago,
Heckled and herded through the fair days too.
This barrel of a man penned in the frame:
I see him with the jaunty hat pushed back
Draw thumbs out of his waistcoat, curtly smack
Hands and sell. Father, I've watched you do the same

And watched you sadden when the fairs were stopped.
No room for dealers if the farmers shopped
Like housewives at an auction ring. Your stick
Was parked behind the door and stands there still.
Closing this chapter of our chronicle,
I take your uncle's portrait to the attic.

Mid-Term Break

I sat all morning in the college sick bay,
Counting bells knelling classes to a close.
At two o'clock our neighbours drove me home.

In the porch I met my father crying —
He had always taken funerals in his stride —
And Big Jim Evans saying it was a hard blow.

The baby cooed and laughed and rocked the pram
When I came in, and I was embarrassed
By old men standing up to shake my hand

And tell me they were 'sorry for my trouble'.
Whispers informed strangers I was the eldest,
Away at school, as my mother held my hand

In hers and coughed out angry tearless sighs.
At ten o'clock the ambulance arrived
With the corpse, stanched and bandaged by the nurses.

Next morning I went up into the room. Snowdrops
And candles soothed the bedside; I saw him
For the first time in six weeks. Paler now,

Wearing a poppy bruise on his left temple,
He lay in the four foot box as in his cot.
No gaudy scars, the bumper knocked him clear.

A four foot box, a foot for every year.

Dawn Shoot

Clouds ran their wet mortar, plastered the daybreak
Grey. The stones clicked tartly
If we missed the sleepers, but mostly
Silent we headed up the railway
Where now the only steam was funnelling from cows
Ditched on their rumps beyond hedges,
Cudding, watching, and knowing.
The rails scored a bull's-eye into the eye
Of a bridge. A corncrake challenged
Unexpectedly like a hoarse sentry
And a snipe rocketed away on reconnaissance.
Rubber-booted, belted, tense as two parachutists,
We climbed the iron gate and dropped
Into the meadow's six acres of broom, gorse and dew.

A sandy bank, reinforced with coiling roots,
Faced you, two hundred yards from the track.
Snug on our bellies behind a rise of dead whins,
Our ravenous eyes getting used to the greyness,
We settled, soon had the holes under cover.
This was the den they all would be heading for now,
Loping under ferns in dry drains, flashing
Brown orbits across ploughlands and grazing.

The plaster thinned at the skyline, the whitewash
Was bleaching on houses and stables,
The cock would be sounding reveille

In seconds.
And there was one breaking
In from the gap in the corner.

Donnelly's left hand came up
And came down on my barrel. This one was his,
'For Christ's sake,' I spat, 'Take your time, there'll be
    more.'
There was the playboy trotting up to the hole
By the ash tree, 'Wild rover no more,'
Said Donnelly and emptied two barrels
And got him.

Another snipe catapulted into the light,
A mare whinnied and shivered her haunches
Up on a hill. The others would not be back
After three shots like that. We dandered off
To the railway; the prices were small at that time
So we did not bother to cut out the tongue.
The ones that slipped back when the all clear got
    round
Would be first to examine him.

At a Potato Digging

I

A mechanical digger wrecks the drill,
Spins up a dark shower of roots and mould.
Labourers swarm in behind, stoop to fill
Wicker creels. Fingers go dead in the cold.

Like crows attacking crow-black fields, they stretch
A higgledy line from hedge to headland;
Some pairs keep breaking ragged ranks to fetch
A full creel to the pit and straighten, stand

Tall for a moment but soon stumble back
To fish a new load from the crumbled surf.
Heads bow, trunks bend, hands fumble towards the
   black
Mother. Processional stooping through the turf

Recurs mindlessly as autumn. Centuries
Of fear and homage to the famine god
Toughen the muscles behind their humbled knees,
Make a seasonal altar of the sod.

II

Flint-white, purple. They lie scattered
like inflated pebbles. Native
to the black hutch of clay

where the halved seed shot and clotted,
these knobbed and slit-eyed tubers seem
the petrified hearts of drills. Split
by the spade, they show white as cream.

Good smells exude from crumbled earth.
The rough bark of humus erupts
knots of potatoes (a clean birth)
whose solid feel, whose wet insides
promise taste of ground and root.
To be piled in pits; live skulls, blind-eyed.

III

Live skulls, blind-eyed, balanced on
wild higgledy skeletons,
scoured the land in 'forty-five,
wolfed the blighted root and died.

The new potato, sound as stone,
putrefied when it had lain
three days in the long clay pit.
Millions rotted along with it.

Mouths tightened in, eyes died hard,
faces chilled to a plucked bird.
In a million wicker huts,
beaks of famine snipped at guts.

A people hungering from birth,
grubbing, like plants, in the earth,

were grafted with a great sorrow.
Hope rotted like a marrow.

Stinking potatoes fouled the land,
pits turned pus into filthy mounds:
and where potato diggers are,
you still smell the running sore.

IV

Under a gay flotilla of gulls
The rhythm deadens, the workers stop.
Brown bread and tea in bright canfuls
Are served for lunch. Dead-beat, they flop

Down in the ditch and take their fill,
Thankfully breaking timeless fasts;
Then, stretched on the faithless ground, spill
Libations of cold tea, scatter crusts.

For the Commander of the *Eliza*

*. . . the others, with emaciated faces and prominent, staring
eyeballs, were evidently in an advanced state of starvation. The
officer reported to Sir James Dombrain . . . and Sir James, 'very
inconveniently', wrote Routh, 'interfered'.*

CECIL WOODHAM-SMITH: THE GREAT HUNGER

Routine patrol off West Mayo; sighting
A rowboat heading unusually far
Beyond the creek, I tacked and hailed the crew
In Gaelic. Their stroke had clearly weakened
As they pulled to, from guilt or bashfulness
I was conjecturing when, O my sweet Christ,
We saw piled in the bottom of their craft
Six grown men with gaping mouths and eyes
Bursting the sockets like spring onions in drills.
Six wrecks of bone and pallid, tautened skin.
'Bia, bia,
Bia'. In whines and snarls their desperation
Rose and fell like a flock of starving gulls.
We'd known about the shortage, but on board
They always kept us right with flour and beef
So understand my feelings, and the men's,
Who had no mandate to relieve distress
Since relief was then available in Westport –
Though clearly these poor brutes would never make it.
I had to refuse food: they cursed and howled
Like dogs that had been kicked hard in the privates.
When they drove at me with their starboard oar
(Risking capsize themselves) I saw they were
Violent and without hope. I hoisted
And cleared off. Less incidents the better.

[21]

Next day, like six bad smells, those living skulls
Drifted through the dark of bunks and hatches
And once in port I exorcised my ship,
Reporting all to the Inspector General.
Sir James, I understand, urged free relief
For famine victims in the Westport Sector
And earned tart reprimand from good Whitehall.
Let natives prosper by their own exertions;
Who could not swim might go ahead and sink.
'The Coast Guard with their zeal and activity
Are too lavish' were the words, I think.

The Diviner

Cut from the green hedge a forked hazel stick
That he held tight by the arms of the V:
Circling the terrain, hunting the pluck
Of water, nervous, but professionally

Unfussed. The pluck came sharp as a sting.
The rod jerked with precise convulsions,
Spring water suddenly broadcasting
Through a green hazel its secret stations.

The bystanders would ask to have a try.
He handed them the rod without a word.
It lay dead in their grasp till, nonchalantly,
He gripped expectant wrists. The hazel stirred.

Turkeys Observed

One observes them, one expects them;
Blue-breasted in their indifferent mortuary,
Beached bare on the cold marble slabs
In immodest underwear frills of feather.

The red sides of beef retain
Some of the smelly majesty of living:
A half-cow slung from a hook maintains
That blood and flesh are not ignored.

But a turkey cowers in death.
Pull his neck, pluck him, and look —
He is just another poor forked thing,
A skin bag plumped with inky putty.

He once complained extravagantly
In an overture of gobbles;
He lorded it on the claw-flecked mud
With a grey flick of his Confucian eye.

Now, as I pass the bleak Christmas dazzle,
I find him ranged with his cold squadrons:
The fuselage is bare, the proud wings snapped,
The tail-fan stripped down to a shameful rudder.

Cow in Calf

It seems she has swallowed a barrel.
From forelegs to haunches,
her belly is slung like a hammock.

Slapping her out of the byre is like slapping
a great bag of seed. My hand
tingled as if strapped, but I had to
hit her again and again and
heard the blows plump like a depth-charge
far in her gut.

The udder grows. Windbags
of bagpipes are crammed there
to drone in her lowing.
Her cud and her milk, her heats and her calves
keep coming and going.

Trout

Hangs, a fat gun-barrel,
deep under arched bridges
or slips like butter down
the throat of the river.

From depths smooth-skinned as plums,
his muzzle gets bull's eye;
picks off grass-seed and moths
that vanish, torpedoed.

Where water unravels
over gravel-beds he
is fired from the shallows,
white belly reporting

flat; darts like a tracer-
bullet back between stones
and is never burnt out.
A volley of cold blood

ramrodding the current.

Waterfall

The burn drowns steadily in its own downpour,
A helter-skelter of muslin and glass
That skids to a halt, crashing up suds.

Simultaneous acceleration
And sudden braking; water goes over
Like villains dropped screaming to justice.

It appears an athletic glacier
Has reared into reverse: is swallowed up
And regurgitated through this long throat.

My eye rides over and downwards, falls with
Hurtling tons that slabber and spill,
Falls, yet records the tumult thus standing still.

Docker

There, in the corner, staring at his drink.
The cap juts like a gantry's crossbeam,
Cowling plated forehead and sledgehead jaw.
Speech is clamped in the lips' vice.

That fist would drop a hammer on a Catholic —
Oh yes, that kind of thing could start again.
The only Roman collar he tolerates
Smiles all round his sleek pint of porter.

Mosaic imperatives bang home like rivets;
God is a foreman with certain definite views
Who orders life in shifts of work and leisure.
A factory horn will blare the Resurrection.

He sits, strong and blunt as a Celtic cross,
Clearly used to silence and an armchair:
Tonight the wife and children will be quiet
At slammed door and smoker's cough in the hall.

Poor Women in a City Church

The small wax candles melt to light,
Flicker in marble, reflect bright
Asterisks on brass candlesticks:
At the Virgin's altar on the right,
Blue flames are jerking on wicks.

Old dough-faced women with black shawls
Drawn down tight kneel in the stalls.
Cold yellow candle-tongues, blue flame
Mince and caper as whispered calls
Take wing up to the Holy Name.

Thus each day in the sacred place
They kneel. Golden shrines, altar lace,
Marble columns and cool shadows
Still them. In the gloom you cannot trace
A wrinkle on their beeswax brows.

Gravities

High-riding kites appear to range quite freely,
Though reined by strings, strict and invisible.
The pigeon that deserts you suddenly
Is heading home, instinctively faithful.

Lovers with barrages of hot insult
Often cut off their nose to spite their face,
Endure a hopeless day, declare their guilt,
Re-enter the native port of their embrace.

Blinding in Paris, for his party-piece
Joyce named the shops along O'Connell Street
And on Iona Colmcille sought ease
By wearing Irish mould next to his feet.

Twice Shy

Her scarf *à la* Bardot,
In suede flats for the walk,
She came with me one evening
For air and friendly talk.
We crossed the quiet river,
Took the embankment walk.

Traffic holding its breath,
Sky a tense diaphragm:
Dusk hung like a backcloth
That shook where a swan swam,
Tremulous as a hawk
Hanging deadly, calm.

A vacuum of need
Collapsed each hunting heart
But tremulously we held
As hawk and prey apart,
Preserved classic decorum,
Deployed our talk with art.

Our juvenilia
Had taught us both to wait,
Not to publish feeling
And regret it all too late –
Mushroom loves already
Had puffed and burst in hate.

So, chary and excited
As a thrush linked on a hawk,
We thrilled to the March twilight
With nervous childish talk:
Still waters running deep
Along the embankment walk.

Valediction

Lady with the frilled blouse
And simple tartan skirt,
Since you left the house
Its emptiness has hurt
All thought. In your presence
Time rode easy, anchored
On a smile; but absence
Rocked love's balance, unmoored
The days. They buck and bound
Across the calendar,
Pitched from the quiet sound
Of your flower-tender
Voice. Need breaks on my strand;
You've gone, I am at sea.
Until you resume command,
Self is in mutiny.

Lovers on Aran

The timeless waves, bright, sifting, broken glass,
Came dazzling around, into the rocks,
Came glinting, sifting from the Americas

To possess Aran. Or did Aran rush
To throw wide arms of rock around a tide
That yielded with an ebb, with a soft crash?

Did sea define the land or land the sea?
Each drew new meaning from the waves' collision.
Sea broke on land to full identity.

Poem

For Marie

Love, I shall perfect for you the child
Who diligently potters in my brain
Digging with heavy spade till sods were piled
Or puddling through muck in a deep drain.

Yearly I would sow my yard-long garden.
I'd strip a layer of sods to build the wall
That was to exclude sow and pecking hen.
Yearly, admitting these, the sods would fall.

Or in the sucking clabber I would splash
Delightedly and dam the flowing drain,
But always my bastions of clay and mush
Would burst before the rising autumn rain.

Love, you shall perfect for me this child
Whose small imperfect limits would keep breaking:
Within new limits now, arrange the world
Within our walls, within our golden ring.

Honeymoon Flight

Below, the patchwork earth, dark hems of hedge,
The long grey tapes of road that bind and loose
Villages and fields in casual marriage:
We bank above the small lough and farmhouse

And the sure green world goes topsy-turvy
As we climb out of our familiar landscape.
The engine noises change. You look at me.
The coastline slips away beneath the wing-tip.

And launched right off the earth by force of fire,
We hang, miraculous, above the water,
Dependent on the invisible air
To keep us airborne and to bring us further.

Ahead of us the sky's a geyser now.
A calm voice talks of cloud yet we feel lost.
Air-pockets jolt our fears and down we go.
Travellers, at this point, can only trust.

Scaffolding

Masons, when they start upon a building,
Are careful to test out the scaffolding;

Make sure that planks won't slip at busy points,
Secure all ladders, tighten bolted joints.

And yet all this comes down when the job's done,
Showing off walls of sure and solid stone.

So if, my dear, there sometimes seem to be
Old bridges breaking between you and me,

Never fear. We may let the scaffolds fall,
Confident that we have built our wall.

Storm on the Island

We are prepared: we build our houses squat,
Sink walls in rock and roof them with good slate.
This wizened earth has never troubled us
With hay, so, as you see, there are no stacks
Or stooks that can be lost. Nor are there trees
Which might prove company when it blows full
Blast: you know what I mean – leaves and branches
Can raise a tragic chorus in a gale
So that you listen to the thing you fear
Forgetting that it pummels your house too.
But there are no trees, no natural shelter.
You might think that the sea is company,
Exploding comfortably down on the cliffs,
But no: when it begins, the flung spray hits
The very windows, spits like a tame cat
Turned savage. We just sit tight while wind dives
And strafes invisibly. Space is a salvo,
We are bombarded by the empty air.
Strange, it is a huge nothing that we fear.

Synge on Aran

Salt off the sea whets
the blades of four winds.
They peel acres
of locked rock, pare down
a rind of shrivelled ground;
bull-noses are chiselled
on cliffs.
                    Islanders too
are for sculpting. Note
the pointed scowl, the mouth
carved as upturned anchor
and the polished head
full of drownings.
                              There
he comes now, a hard pen
scraping in his head;
the nib filed on a salt wind
and dipped in the keening sea.

Saint Francis and the Birds

When Francis preached love to the birds,
They listened, fluttered, throttled up
Into the blue like a flock of words

Released for fun from his holy lips.
Then wheeled back, whirred about his head,
Pirouetted on brothers' capes,

Danced on the wing, for sheer joy played
And sang, like images took flight.
Which was the best poem Francis made,

His argument true, his tone light.

In Small Townlands

For Colin Middleton

In small townlands his hogshair wedge
Will split the granite from the clay
Till crystal in the rock is bared:
Loaded brushes hone an edge
On mountain blue and heather grey.
Outcrops of stone contract, outstared.

The spectrum bursts, a bright grenade,
When he unlocks the safety catch
On morning dew, on cloud, on rain.
The splintered lights slice like a spade
That strips the land of fuzz and blotch,
Pares clean as bone, cruel as the pain

That strikes in a wild heart attack.
His eyes, thick, greedy lenses, fire
This bare bald earth with white and red,
Incinerate it till it's black
And brilliant as a funeral pyre:
A new world cools out of his head.

The Folk Singers

Re-turning time-turned words,
Fitting each weathered song
To a new-grooved harmony,
They pluck slick strings and swing
A sad heart's equilibrium.

Numb passion, pearled in the shy
Shell of a country love
And strung on a frail tune,
Looks sharp now, strikes a pose
Like any rustic new to the bright town.

Their pre-packed tale will sell
Ten thousand times: pale love
Rouged for the streets. Humming
Solders all broken hearts. Death's edge
Blunts on the narcotic strumming.

The Play Way

Sunlight pillars through glass, probes each desk
For milk-tops, drinking straws and old dry crusts.
The music strides to challenge it,
Mixing memory and desire with chalk dust.

My lesson notes read: *Teacher will play*
Beethoven's Concerto Number Five
And class will express themselves freely
In writing. One said 'Can we jive?'

When I produced the record, but now
The big sound has silenced them. Higher
And firmer, each authoritative note
Pumps the classroom up tight as a tyre,

Working its private spell behind eyes
That stare wide. They have forgotten me
For once. The pens are busy, the tongues mime
Their blundering embrace of the free

Word. A silence charged with sweetness
Breaks short on lost faces where I see
New looks. Then notes stretch taut as snares. They trip
To fall into themselves unknowingly.

Personal Helicon

For Michael Longley

As a child, they could not keep me from wells
And old pumps with buckets and windlasses.
I loved the dark drop, the trapped sky, the smells
Of waterweed, fungus and dank moss.

One, in a brickyard, with a rotted board top.
I savoured the rich crash when a bucket
Plummeted down at the end of a rope.
So deep you saw no reflection in it.

A shallow one under a dry stone ditch
Fructified like any aquarium.
When you dragged out long roots from the soft mulch,
A white face hovered over the bottom.

Others had echoes, gave back your own call
With a clean new music in it. And one
Was scaresome for there, out of ferns and tall
Foxgloves, a rat slapped across my reflection.

Now, to pry into roots, to finger slime,
To stare, big-eyed Narcissus, into some spring
Is beneath all adult dignity. I rhyme
To see myself, to set the darkness echoing.